THE
Serial
Killer
COLORING BOOK

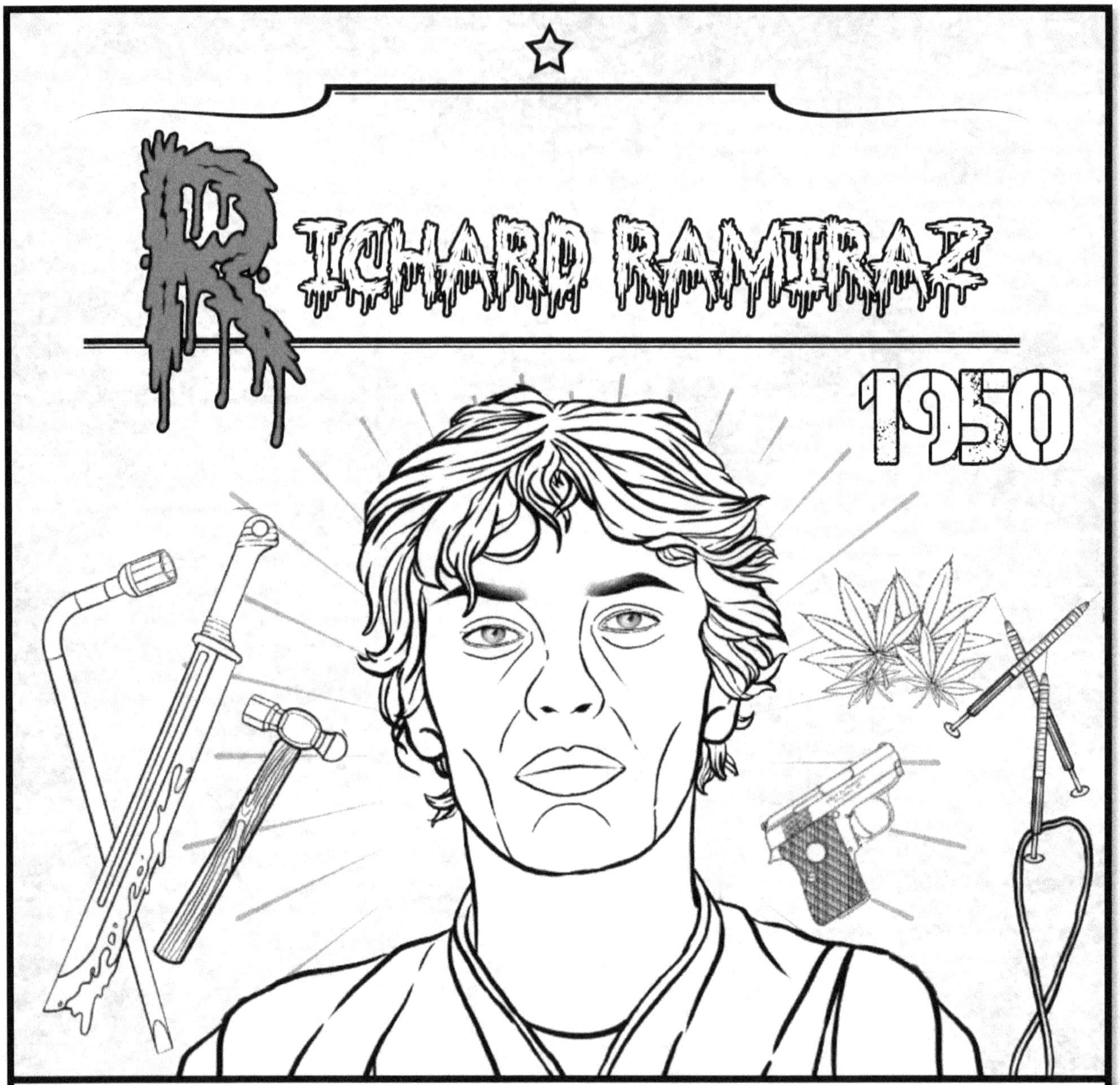

THIS COLORING BOOK BELONGS TO

....

COLOR TEST

DENNIS RADER
1945
Christ Lutheran Church
NICKNAME : THE BTK KILLER
UNITED STATE

H H. HOLMES
1861
NICKNAME : BEAST OF CHICAGO
UNITED STATE

JOSEF NASO
1934
Diary
JOSEPH
NASO
MY VICTIM
JOSEPH
QUOTE : "I DON'T KILL PEOPLE"
UNITED STATE

RICHARD RAMIRAZ

1950

NICKNAME : THE NIGHT STALKER

UNITED STATE

ALBERT DESAYLO
1931
QUOTE : "I HAD A LOT OF FUN .. KILLING SOMBODY'S"
UNITED STATE

KRISTEN GILBERT
1967
Intravenous therapy IV
500ml
THERE'S A BOMB IN THE HOSPITAL!
Epinephrine
Angel of death
NICKNAME : THE ANGEL OF DEATH
UNITED STATE

DAVID PARKER RAY
1939
NICKNAME : THE TOY-BOX KILLER
UNITED STATE

JOSEPH PAUL FRANKLIN
1950
NICKNAME : THE RACIST KILLER
UNITED STATE

LEONARD THOMAS LAKE

QIOTE : "I WANT TO BE ABLE TO USE A WOMEN WHENEVER AND HOWEVER I WANT"

UNITED STATE

EDMUND KEMPER
1948
NICKNAME : CO-ED BUTCHER
UNITED STATE

CARL PANZRAM

1892

QUOTE : "I BELIEVE THAT THE ONE WAY TO REFORM PEOPLE IS TO KILL'EM"

UNITED STATE

DAVID BEAKOWITZ
1953
QUOTE : "MY PARENTS COULDN'T REACH ME, NOT EVEN WITH ALL OF THEIR LOVE"
UNITED STATE

KARLA HOMOLKA

1970

NICKNAME : THE WITCH OF ONTARIO

CANADA

JOEL RIFKIN
1959
PAI
NICKNAME : JOEL THE RIPPER
UNITED STATE

WILLIAM BONIN
1947
HYDROCHLORIC ACID
TEQUILA
QUOTE : "I COULDN'T STOP THE KILLING IT GOT EASIER EACH TIME"
UNITED STATE

GARY M. HEIDNIK
1943
United Church of the Ministers of God
$
NICKNAME : BROTHER BISHOP
UNITED STATE

ED GEIN
1906
QUOTE : "SHE ISN'T MISSING.
SHE'S AT THE FARM RIGHT NOW"
UNITED STATE
Old School
Old School

ROBERT LEE YATES
1952
BRANDY
BRANDY
VODKA
BEER
NICKNAME : SPOKANE WASHINGTON'S
SERIAL KILLER
UNITED STATE

DEAN CORLL
1939
NICKNAME : THE CANDY MAN
UNITED STATE

HENRY LEE LUCAS
1936
Old School
NICKNAME : THE DEADLY DRIFTER
UNITED STATE
Old School

LONNIE FRANKLIN JR
1952
NICKNAME : GRIM SLEEPER
UNITED STATE

RICHARD COTTINGHAM

1946

NICKNAME : THE TORSO KILLER

UNITED STATE

KEITH HUNTER JESPERSON

1955

NICKNAME : HAPPY FACE KILLER

UNITED STATE

MARYBETH TINNING
ARRESTED: FEBRUARY 5, 1986
Marybeth Tinning
Serial killer mom
Schenectady, New York
1942
9
Innocent lives
QUOTE : "I SMOTHERED THEM EACH WITH A
PILLOW BECAUSE I'M NOT A GOOD MOTHER
UNITED STATE

ROBERT HANSEN
1939
NICKNAME : THE BUTCHER BAKER
UNITED STAT

AILEEN WUORNOS
1956
NICKNAME : DAMSEL OF DEATH
UNITED STAT

PAUL JOHN KNOWLES

1946

NICKNAME : THE CASANOVA KILLER

UNITED STAT

NANNIE DOSS
1905
Art of Love
When Lightning Strikes
The Side of Paradise
The Hawk of Venice
DAILY NEW
LONELY HEART
COLUMN
Romance
Arsenic
PRICE
POISON
10 CTS.
Rat killer
NICKNAME : LADY BLUE BEARD,
BLACK WIDOW
UNITED STATE

JEFFREY DAHMER
1960
Soilex
SOILEX SUPER WASH
5 Kgs.
NICKNAME : MILWAUKEE CANNIBAL
UNITED STATE

GARY RIDGWAY
1949
SERIAL KILLER
QUOTE : "I ALWAYS WONDRED WHAT IT WOULD BE LIKE TO KILL SOMEONE"
UNITED STATE

ARTHUR SHAWCROSS
1945
NICKNAME : THE GENESEE RIVER KILLER
UNITED STAT

KENNETH BIANCHI
1951
Windex
MULTI-SURFACE
NICKNAME : HILLSIDE STRANGLER
UNITED STAT

RANDY STEVEN KRAFT

1945

NICKNAME : SCORECARD KILLER

UNITED STAT

CPSIA information can be obtained
at www.ICGtesting.com
Printed in the USA
LVHW061154120622
721085LV00023B/532

9 798711 778462